Before They Were President

BEFORE DONALD TRUMP WAS PRESIDENT

By Ryan Nagelhout

Gareth Stevens
PUBLISHING

Please visit our website, www.garethstevens.com. For a free color catalog of all our high-quality books, call toll free 1-800-542-2595 or fax 1-877-542-2596.

Cataloging-in-Publication Data

Names: Nagelhout, Ryan.
Title: Before Donald Trump was president / Ryan Nagelhout.
Description: New York : Gareth Stevens Publishing, 2018. | Series: Before they were president | Includes index.
Identifiers: ISBN 9781538210642 (pbk.) | ISBN 9781538210666 (library bound) | ISBN 9781538210659 (6 pack)
Subjects: LCSH: Trump, Donald, 1946–Juvenile literature. | Presidents–United States–Biography–Juvenile literature.
Classification: LCC E911.N34 2018 | DDC 973.933092–dc23

First Edition

Published in 2018 by
Gareth Stevens Publishing
111 East 14th Street, Suite 349
New York, NY 10003

Copyright © 2018 Gareth Stevens Publishing

Designer: Laura Bowen
Editor: Ryan Nagelhout/Kate Mikoley

Photo credits: Cover, p. 1 (Donald Trump) Pool/Getty Images News/Getty Images; cover, p. 1 (New York City) kropic1/Shutterstock.com; cover, pp. 1–21 (frame) Samran wonglakorn/Shutterstock.com; p. 5 (main) FloridaStock/ Shutterstock.com; p. 5 (inset) DON EMMERT/AFP/Getty Images; p. 7 Quibik/Wikimedia Commons; p. 9 Ron Galella/ Ron Galella Collection/Getty Images; p. 11 (main) Joe McNally/Hulton Archive/Getty Images; p. 11 (inset) Phototasty/ Shutterstock.com; p. 13 AFP/Stringer/Getty Images; p. 15 (top) Spencer Platt/Getty Images News/Getty Images; p. 15 (bottom) Mark Wilson/Getty Images News/Getty Images; p. 17 Mathew Imaging/FilmMagic/Getty Images; p. 19 OLOS/Shutterstock.com; p. 21 (top) SAUL LOEB/AFP/Getty Images; p. 21 (bottom) Smartyllama/Wikimedia Commons.

Printed in China

CPSIA compliance information: Batch #CW18GS: For further information contact Gareth Stevens, New York, New York at 1-800-542-2595.

CONTENTS

Words in the glossary appear in **bold** type the first time they are used in the text.

THE WINTER WHITE HOUSE

In 1985, Donald Trump bought a large house called Mar-a-Lago in Palm Beach, Florida. Once the home of a wealthy woman who loved to have parties, it became known as the "Winter White House" after Trump was elected president in 2016.

In fact, Trump's business of buying and selling land and buildings is one reason people elected him president. So let's find out what Trump did before he became the 45th president of the United States. It's time to learn more about young Donald Trump.

Presidential Preview

Mar-a-Lago's builder, Marjorie Merriweather Post, hoped the house might one day be a getaway for presidents who wanted to spend time away from Washington, DC. She gave it to the nation when she died, but no president wanted to use it. Today, a president owns it!

TRUMP AT MAR-A-LAGO

MANY PRESIDENTS STILL SPEND TIME AT THEIR OWN HOMES. LIKE TRUMP'S MAR-A-LAGO, GEORGE WASHINGTON'S MOUNT VERNON, OR GEORGE W. BUSH'S RANCH IN CRAWFORD, TEXAS, IT'S COMMON FOR PRESIDENTS TO HAVE SECOND HOMES WHILE IN OFFICE.

FAMILY MONEY

Donald John Trump was born on June 14, 1946, in Queens, New York. Donald was the fourth of five children of Frederick and Mary MacLeod Trump. His father worked in real estate, or the buying and selling of property. Fred Trump built and owned apartments in Queens, Staten Island, and Brooklyn in New York City.

Trump was high-spirited as a child and was sent to the New York Military Academy when he was 13. His parents hoped he would learn **discipline** there.

Presidential Preview

Donald's family was very wealthy. When Trump started his own business, Fred Trump was worth nearly $200 million!

DONALD HAD FOUR SIBLINGS—TWO BROTHERS, FRED JR. AND ROBERT, AND TWO SISTERS, ELIZABETH AND MARYANNE.

YOUNG DONALD TRUMP

SCHOOL AND BUSINESS

Trump graduated from the military academy in 1964. He attended college at Fordham **University** for 2 years, then went to the Wharton School at the University of Pennsylvania. Trump graduated in 1968 with a **degree** in economics.

While he was in school, Trump worked for his father's real estate business, Elizabeth Trump & Son. After he graduated, he joined the business full time. In 1971, he was given control of the company, which he renamed the Trump Organization.

Presidential Preview

Though he went to a military school before college, Trump didn't join the military and fight in the Vietnam War (1955–1975). Trump received **deferments** during and after college.

TRUMP HAD BIG PLANS FOR HIS FATHER'S BUSINESS, WHICH MOSTLY BUILT AND OWNED HOUSING IN NEW YORK CITY. HE BOUGHT PROPERTY IN PHILADELPHIA, PENNSYLVANIA, WHILE HE WAS AT WHARTON.

DONALD AND FRED TRUMP

TRUMP TOWER

Trump moved to Manhattan, a part of New York City, and his company became part of major building projects there. Trump worked to open hotels and improve buildings around the city, making his company money and making himself well known throughout the country.

Trump named many of his projects after himself, including Trump Parc, Trump Palace, and Trump Plaza. One of Trump's most famous buildings opened in New York City in 1983—the 58-story Trump Tower. Trump soon moved into the tower himself.

Presidential Preview

Trump Tower in New York City is 664 feet (202 m) tall. But it's not the tallest building with Trump's name on it. The Trump International Hotel and Tower in Chicago, Illinois, is about 1,388 feet (423 m) tall.

TRUMP TOWER

TRUMP AND OTHER MEMBERS OF HIS FAMILY HAVE LIVED AT TRUMP TOWER SINCE IT WAS BUILT IN THE 1980s.

ATLANTIC CITY AND BEYOND

Trump's business grew to include hotels and other properties all around the world. Trump built **casinos** in Atlantic City, New Jersey, and bought Mar-a-Lago in 1985. The Trump Organization has also built golf courses all around the United States and in other nations such as Scotland, the United Arab Emirates, and Ireland.

Trump's hotels can be found in many major cities, including Chicago, Illinois; Las Vegas, Nevada; and Washington, DC. Trump has said that his real estate **portfolio** has made him worth billions of dollars!

Presidential Preview

Trump even owned an airline! He bought an airline for $365 million in 1989. He renamed it Trump Shuttle, Inc., but the company did not make money and came to an end in 1992.

TRUMP LOVES TO GOLF. HE OFTEN GOLFS WITH ATHLETES AND POLITICIANS ON COURSES HE OWNS.

13

A FAMILY MAN

Donald Trump married his first wife, Ivana Zelníčková, in 1977. Trump had three children while married to Ivana—two sons, Donald Jr. and Eric, and a daughter, Ivanka.

Trump had another daughter, Tiffany, with his second wife, Marla Maples. In 2005, Trump married his third wife, Melania Knauss. They had a son, Barron, a year later. Trump is close to his five children—Donald Jr. and Eric took over the family business when he became president.

Presidential Preview

In 1987, Trump cowrote a book called *Trump: The Art of the Deal*. It was very popular and is just one of many books Trump has worked on.

TIFFANY, ERIC, IVANKA, DONALD JR., MELANIA, AND DONALD

IVANKA TRUMP AND HER HUSBAND, JARED KUSHNER, ARE PART OF TRUMP'S STAFF AT THE WHITE HOUSE.

BARRON AND DONALD TRUMP

15

FIRING ON TV

Trump showed America his business sense through a reality television show called *The Apprentice*. On the show, business people competed to finish tasks and **impress** Trump. The person who did the worst would be "fired" by Trump. The person who did the best might be hired by Trump. The show started in 2004, and Trump was the host for 14 seasons.

The show even helped him find people to work in the White House once he became president! Omarosa Manigault, who appeared on *The Apprentice* in 2004, became part of Trump's staff in 2017.

Presidential Preview

Trump often appeared on other TV shows over the years, including cable news shows. Many of these interviews he did by phone.

America learned more about Trump and his business through a "reality competition" television show, a kind of TV show where real people are filmed as they try to win a game.

TRUMP THE BRAND

Along with his hotels, casinos, and golf courses, Trump has put his name on steaks, bottled water, and furniture. He even had his own scent—Donald Trump: The Fragrance.

His wife Melania and daughter Ivanka also have their name on products. But not every deal has worked out. Several Trump-named properties, including casinos in Atlantic City, have gone **bankrupt**, and several Trump-named products, including Trump Steaks and *Trump* magazine, are no longer sold.

Presidential Preview

Trump was **sued** by people who paid money to go to Trump University, a business school he opened in 2005. More than 6,000 "Trump U" students got money back from the university.

Trump Steaks and Trump University weren't hits with the public, but many of his hotels and golf courses remain popular around the world.

TRUMP HOTEL IN LAS VEGAS, NEVADA

RISE TO POWER

On June 16, 2015, Donald Trump declared his bid for United States president. Over the next 17 months, Trump beat out 16 other Republicans to win the party's **nomination**. By stirring national pride and promising more jobs and increased national security, Trump won the presidency over Democratic nominee Hillary Clinton.

Trump is a **controversial** president who brought his business sense to the White House. His surprise campaign broke many presidential **traditions** and rules, and his presidency is sure to do the same!

Presidential Preview

Though Trump once thought of himself as a Democrat, he later became a Republican and got the party's nomination for the 2016 election. He was also part of the Reform Party in the 1980s.

Trump's Timeline

1946 Donald John Trump is born on June 14.

1959 Trump attends New York Military Academy.

1966 Trump transfers from Fordham to the Wharton School at the University of Pennsylvania.

1977 Trump marries his first wife, Ivana Zělníčková. Donald Jr. is born on December 31.

1981 Ivanka is born on October 30.

1983 Trump Tower opens in New York City in February.

1984 Eric is born on January 6.

1985 Trump buys Mar-a-Lago in Palm Beach, Florida.

1987 Trump publishes *Trump: The Art of the Deal*.

1993 Tiffany is born on October 13. Trump marries his second wife, Marla Maples, in December.

2004 *The Apprentice* airs on NBC.

2005 Trump marries his third wife, Melania Knauss. Trump University opens.

2006 Barron is born on March 20.

2015 Trump announces his bid for presidency on June 16.

2016 Trump wins the election on November 8.

2017 Trump is sworn in as 45th president on January 20.

DONALD, BARRON, AND MELANIA

PRESIDENT TRUMP

GLOSSARY

apprentice: someone who learns a job by working with a skilled person of that trade

bankrupt: unable to pay back money owed

casino: a place where people play games of chance

controversial: something many people disagree about

deferment: putting something off for a later time, like military service

degree: a title given to a student for finishing school

discipline: a type of conduct that includes following rules and practicing self-control

impress: to gain another's interest

nomination: the act of choosing someone to run for office

portfolio: the total collection of properties or other things worth money

sue: to seek justice from a person by bringing a lawful action

tradition: having to do with long-practiced ways of doing something

university: a school for higher learning

FOR MORE INFORMATION

Books

Gimpel, Diane Marczely. *Donald Trump*. Mankato, MN: Child's World, 2017.

Lee, Jake. *Donald Trump: 45th President*. Minneapolis, MN: ABDO Publishing, 2017.

Sherman, Jill. *Donald Trump: Outspoken Personality and President*. Minneapolis, MN: Lerner Publications, 2017.

Websites

Donald Trump

ducksters.com/biography/uspresidents/donaldtrump.php
Find out more facts about Trump here.

President Donald J. Trump

whitehouse.gov/administration/president-trump
Here's Trump's official White House biography.

INDEX